This Log Book Belongs to:

_____

_____

_____

Date: _____

Departure Location	Departure Time
Stopover	Time
Arrival Location	Date & Time

Wind Direction	Wind Speed
Coordinates	Temperature
Waves	Sky
Forecast	Motoring
Fuel	Water
Captain	Engine Hours

Sea Strength: Calm — 1 2 3 4 5 — Rough

Crew

Notes

Logged By: _____

Date: _____

Departure Location	Departure Time
Stopover	Time
Arrival Location	Date & Time

Wind Direction	Wind Speed
Coordinates	Temperature
Waves	Sky
Forecast	Motoring
Fuel	Water
Captain	Engine Hours

Sea Strength: Calm ●——| 1 | 2 | 3 | 4 | 5 |——● Rough

Crew

Notes

Logged By: _____

Date:

Departure Location	Departure Time
Stopover	Time
Arrival Location	Date & Time

Wind Direction	Wind Speed
Coordinates	Temperature
Waves	Sky
Forecast	Motoring
Fuel	Water
Captain	Engine Hours

Sea Strength: Calm ●——(| 1 | 2 | 3 | 4 | 5 |)——● Rough

Crew

Notes

Logged By:

Date: _____

Departure Location	Departure Time
Stopover	Time
Arrival Location	Date & Time

Wind Direction	Wind Speed
Coordinates	Temperature
Waves	Sky
Forecast	Motoring
Fuel	Water
Captain	Engine Hours

Sea Strength: Calm ●— | 1 | 2 | 3 | 4 | 5 | —● Rough

Crew

Notes

Logged By: _____

Date:

Departure Location	Departure Time
Stopover	Time
Arrival Location	Date & Time

Wind Direction	Wind Speed
Coordinates	Temperature
Waves	Sky
Forecast	Motoring
Fuel	Water
Captain	Engine Hours

Sea Strength: Calm ● | 1 | 2 | 3 | 4 | 5 | ● Rough

Crew

Notes

Logged By:

Date: _____

Departure Location	Departure Time
Stopover	Time
Arrival Location	Date & Time

Wind Direction	Wind Speed
Coordinates	Temperature
Waves	Sky
Forecast	Motoring
Fuel	Water
Captain	Engine Hours

Sea Strength: Calm ●— 1 | 2 | 3 | 4 | 5 —● Rough

Crew

Notes

Logged By: _____

Date: _____

Departure Location	Departure Time
Stopover	Time
Arrival Location	Date & Time

Wind Direction	Wind Speed
Coordinates	Temperature
Waves	Sky
Forecast	Motoring
Fuel	Water
Captain	Engine Hours

Sea Strength: Calm— 1 2 3 4 5 —Rough

Crew

Notes

Logged By: _____

Date: _____

Departure Location	Departure Time
Stopover	Time
Arrival Location	Date & Time

Wind Direction	Wind Speed
Coordinates	Temperature
Waves	Sky
Forecast	Motoring
Fuel	Water
Captain	Engine Hours

Sea Strength: Calm ● — 1 — 2 — 3 — 4 — 5 — ● Rough

Crew

Notes

Logged By: _____

Date: _____

Departure Location	Departure Time
Stopover	Time
Arrival Location	Date & Time

Wind Direction	Wind Speed
Coordinates	Temperature
Waves	Sky
Forecast	Motoring
Fuel	Water
Captain	Engine Hours

Sea Strength: Calm ●——[| 1 | 2 | 3 | 4 | 5 |]——● Rough

Crew

Notes

Logged By: _____

Date: _____

Departure Location	Departure Time
Stopover	Time
Arrival Location	Date & Time

Wind Direction	Wind Speed
Coordinates	Temperature
Waves	Sky
Forecast	Motoring
Fuel	Water
Captain	Engine Hours

Sea Strength: Calm—● 1 2 3 4 5 ●—Rough

Crew

Notes

Logged By: _____

Date:

Departure Location	Departure Time
Stopover	Time
Arrival Location	Date & Time

Wind Direction	Wind Speed
Coordinates	Temperature
Waves	Sky
Forecast	Motoring
Fuel	Water
Captain	Engine Hours

Sea Strength: Calm ● 1 2 3 4 5 ● Rough

Crew

Notes

Logged By:

Date:

Departure Location	Departure Time
Stopover	Time
Arrival Location	Date & Time

Wind Direction	Wind Speed
Coordinates	Temperature
Waves	Sky
Forecast	Motoring
Fuel	Water
Captain	Engine Hours

Sea Strength: Calm ●— 1 | 2 | 3 | 4 | 5 —● Rough

Crew

Notes

Logged By:

Date:

Departure Location	Departure Time
Stopover	Time
Arrival Location	Date & Time

Wind Direction	Wind Speed
Coordinates	Temperature
Waves	Sky
Forecast	Motoring
Fuel	Water
Captain	Engine Hours

Sea Strength: Calm ● — 1 | 2 | 3 | 4 | 5 — ● Rough

Crew

Notes

Logged By:

Date:

Departure Location	Departure Time
Stopover	Time
Arrival Location	Date & Time

Wind Direction	Wind Speed
Coordinates	Temperature
Waves	Sky
Forecast	Motoring
Fuel	Water
Captain	Engine Hours

Sea Strength:　Calm 1 2 3 4 5 Rough

Crew

Notes

Logged By:

Date: _____

Departure Location	Departure Time
Stopover	Time
Arrival Location	Date & Time

Wind Direction	Wind Speed
Coordinates	Temperature
Waves	Sky
Forecast	Motoring
Fuel	Water
Captain	Engine Hours

Sea Strength: Calm —(1 | 2 | 3 | 4 | 5)— Rough

Crew

Notes

Logged By: _____

Date:

Departure Location	Departure Time
Stopover	Time
Arrival Location	Date & Time

Wind Direction	Wind Speed
Coordinates	Temperature
Waves	Sky
Forecast	Motoring
Fuel	Water
Captain	Engine Hours

Sea Strength: Calm — 1 2 3 4 5 — Rough

Crew

Notes

Logged By:

Date: _____

Departure Location	Departure Time
Stopover	Time
Arrival Location	Date & Time

Wind Direction	Wind Speed
Coordinates	Temperature
Waves	Sky
Forecast	Motoring
Fuel	Water
Captain	Engine Hours

Sea Strength: Calm ●——| 1 | 2 | 3 | 4 | 5 |——● Rough

Crew

Notes

Logged By: _____

Date: _____

Departure Location	Departure Time
Stopover	Time
Arrival Location	Date & Time

Wind Direction	Wind Speed
Coordinates	Temperature
Waves	Sky
Forecast	Motoring
Fuel	Water
Captain	Engine Hours

Sea Strength: Calm ●——| 1 | 2 | 3 | 4 | 5 |——● Rough

Crew

Notes

Logged By: _____

Date: _____

Departure Location	Departure Time
Stopover	Time
Arrival Location	Date & Time

Wind Direction	Wind Speed
Coordinates	Temperature
Waves	Sky
Forecast	Motoring
Fuel	Water
Captain	Engine Hours

Sea Strength: Calm ●—— 1 2 3 4 5 ——● Rough

Crew

Notes

Logged By: _____

Date:

Departure Location	Departure Time
Stopover	Time
Arrival Location	Date & Time

Wind Direction	Wind Speed
Coordinates	Temperature
Waves	Sky
Forecast	Motoring
Fuel	Water
Captain	Engine Hours

Sea Strength: Calm ●━━ 1   2   3   4   5 ━━● Rough

Crew

Notes

Logged By:

Date: _____

Departure Location	Departure Time
Stopover	Time
Arrival Location	Date & Time

Wind Direction	Wind Speed
Coordinates	Temperature
Waves	Sky
Forecast	Motoring
Fuel	Water
Captain	Engine Hours

Sea Strength: Calm ●— 1 2 3 4 5 —● Rough

Crew

Notes

Logged By: _____

Date: _____

Departure Location	Departure Time
Stopover	Time
Arrival Location	Date & Time

Wind Direction	Wind Speed
Coordinates	Temperature
Waves	Sky
Forecast	Motoring
Fuel	Water
Captain	Engine Hours

Sea Strength: Calm ●— 1 | 2 | 3 | 4 | 5 —● Rough

Crew

Notes

Logged By: _____

Date: _____

Departure Location	Departure Time
Stopover	Time
Arrival Location	Date & Time

Wind Direction	Wind Speed
Coordinates	Temperature
Waves	Sky
Forecast	Motoring
Fuel	Water
Captain	Engine Hours

Sea Strength: Calm ●—[| 1 | 2 | 3 | 4 | 5 |]—● Rough

Crew

Notes

Logged By: _____

Date: _____

Departure Location	Departure Time
Stopover	Time
Arrival Location	Date & Time

Wind Direction	Wind Speed
Coordinates	Temperature
Waves	Sky
Forecast	Motoring
Fuel	Water
Captain	Engine Hours

Sea Strength: Calm ●—[1 | 2 | 3 | 4 | 5]—● Rough

Crew

Notes

Logged By: _____

Date: _____

Departure Location	Departure Time
Stopover	Time
Arrival Location	Date & Time

Wind Direction	Wind Speed
Coordinates	Temperature
Waves	Sky
Forecast	Motoring
Fuel	Water
Captain	Engine Hours

Sea Strength: Calm ●—— 1 | 2 | 3 | 4 | 5 ——● Rough

Crew

Notes

Logged By: _____

Date: _____

Departure Location	Departure Time
Stopover	Time
Arrival Location	Date & Time

Wind Direction	Wind Speed
Coordinates	Temperature
Waves	Sky
Forecast	Motoring
Fuel	Water
Captain	Engine Hours

Sea Strength: Calm ● — 1 — 2 — 3 — 4 — 5 — ● Rough

Crew

Notes

Logged By: _____

Date: _____

Departure Location	Departure Time
Stopover	Time
Arrival Location	Date & Time

Wind Direction	Wind Speed
Coordinates	Temperature
Waves	Sky
Forecast	Motoring
Fuel	Water
Captain	Engine Hours

Sea Strength: Calm ●———— 1 | 2 | 3 | 4 | 5 ————● Rough

Crew

Notes

Logged By: _____

Date:

Departure Location	Departure Time
Stopover	Time
Arrival Location	Date & Time

Wind Direction	Wind Speed
Coordinates	Temperature
Waves	Sky
Forecast	Motoring
Fuel	Water
Captain	Engine Hours

Sea Strength: Calm — 1 2 3 4 5 — Rough

Crew

Notes

Logged By:

Date:

Departure Location	Departure Time
Stopover	Time
Arrival Location	Date & Time

Wind Direction	Wind Speed
Coordinates	Temperature
Waves	Sky
Forecast	Motoring
Fuel	Water
Captain	Engine Hours

Sea Strength: Calm — 1 2 3 4 5 — Rough

Crew

Notes

Logged By:

Date:

Departure Location	Departure Time
Stopover	Time
Arrival Location	Date & Time

Wind Direction	Wind Speed
Coordinates	Temperature
Waves	Sky
Forecast	Motoring
Fuel	Water
Captain	Engine Hours

Sea Strength: Calm ●———— 1 | 2 | 3 | 4 | 5 ————● Rough

Crew

Notes

Logged By:

Date: _____

Departure Location	Departure Time
Stopover	Time
Arrival Location	Date & Time

Wind Direction	Wind Speed
Coordinates	Temperature
Waves	Sky
Forecast	Motoring
Fuel	Water
Captain	Engine Hours

Sea Strength: Calm ●——[1 | 2 | 3 | 4 | 5]——● Rough

Crew

Notes

Logged By: _____

Date:

Departure Location		Departure Time
Stopover		Time
Arrival Location		Date & Time

Wind Direction	Wind Speed
Coordinates	Temperature
Waves	Sky
Forecast	Motoring
Fuel	Water
Captain	Engine Hours

Sea Strength: Calm ● — | 1 | 2 | 3 | 4 | 5 | — ● Rough

Crew

Notes

Logged By:

Date: _____

Departure Location	Departure Time
Stopover	Time
Arrival Location	Date & Time

Wind Direction	Wind Speed
Coordinates	Temperature
Waves	Sky
Forecast	Motoring
Fuel	Water
Captain	Engine Hours

Sea Strength: Calm ●——[1 | 2 | 3 | 4 | 5]——● Rough

Crew

Notes

Logged By: _____

Date:

Departure Location	Departure Time
Stopover	Time
Arrival Location	Date & Time

Wind Direction	Wind Speed
Coordinates	Temperature
Waves	Sky
Forecast	Motoring
Fuel	Water
Captain	Engine Hours

Sea Strength: Calm ● — 1 | 2 | 3 | 4 | 5 — ● Rough

Crew

Notes

Logged By:

Date: _____

Departure Location	Departure Time
Stopover	Time
Arrival Location	Date & Time

Wind Direction	Wind Speed
Coordinates	Temperature
Waves	Sky
Forecast	Motoring
Fuel	Water
Captain	Engine Hours

Sea Strength: Calm ● 1 2 3 4 5 ● Rough

Crew

Notes

Logged By: _____

Date: _____

Departure Location	Departure Time
Stopover	Time
Arrival Location	Date & Time

Wind Direction	Wind Speed
Coordinates	Temperature
Waves	Sky
Forecast	Motoring
Fuel	Water
Captain	Engine Hours

Sea Strength: Calm ●— 1 2 3 4 5 —● Rough

Crew

Notes

Logged By: _____

Date:

Departure Location	Departure Time
Stopover	Time
Arrival Location	Date & Time

Wind Direction	Wind Speed
Coordinates	Temperature
Waves	Sky
Forecast	Motoring
Fuel	Water
Captain	Engine Hours

Sea Strength: Calm— 1 2 3 4 5 —Rough

Crew

Notes

Logged By:

Date: _____

Departure Location	Departure Time
Stopover	Time
Arrival Location	Date & Time

Wind Direction	Wind Speed
Coordinates	Temperature
Waves	Sky
Forecast	Motoring
Fuel	Water
Captain	Engine Hours

Sea Strength: Calm ● 1 2 3 4 5 ● Rough

Crew

Notes

Logged By: _____

Date: _____

Departure Location	Departure Time
Stopover	Time
Arrival Location	Date & Time

Wind Direction	Wind Speed
Coordinates	Temperature
Waves	Sky
Forecast	Motoring
Fuel	Water
Captain	Engine Hours

Sea Strength: Calm •— 1 | 2 | 3 | 4 | 5 —• Rough

Crew

Notes

Logged By: _____

Date:

Departure Location	Departure Time
Stopover	Time
Arrival Location	Date & Time

Wind Direction	Wind Speed
Coordinates	Temperature
Waves	Sky
Forecast	Motoring
Fuel	Water
Captain	Engine Hours

Sea Strength: Calm ●———| 1 | 2 | 3 | 4 | 5 |———● Rough

Crew

Notes

Logged By:

Date:

Departure Location	Departure Time
Stopover	Time
Arrival Location	Date & Time

Wind Direction	Wind Speed
Coordinates	Temperature
Waves	Sky
Forecast	Motoring
Fuel	Water
Captain	Engine Hours

Sea Strength: Calm — 1 2 3 4 5 — Rough

Crew

Notes

Logged By:

Date:

Departure Location	Departure Time
Stopover	Time
Arrival Location	Date & Time

Wind Direction	Wind Speed
Coordinates	Temperature
Waves	Sky
Forecast	Motoring
Fuel	Water
Captain	Engine Hours

Sea Strength: Calm ● 1 2 3 4 5 ● Rough

Crew

Notes

Logged By:

Date: _____

Departure Location	Departure Time
Stopover	Time
Arrival Location	Date & Time

Wind Direction	Wind Speed
Coordinates	Temperature
Waves	Sky
Forecast	Motoring
Fuel	Water
Captain	Engine Hours

Sea Strength: Calm —○— 1 | 2 | 3 | 4 | 5 —○— Rough

Crew

Notes

Logged By: _____

Date: _____

Departure Location	Departure Time
Stopover	Time
Arrival Location	Date & Time

Wind Direction	Wind Speed
Coordinates	Temperature
Waves	Sky
Forecast	Motoring
Fuel	Water
Captain	Engine Hours

Sea Strength: Calm •———— 1 — 2 — 3 — 4 — 5 ————• Rough

Crew

Notes

Logged By: _____

Date: _____

Departure Location		Departure Time
Stopover		Time
Arrival Location		Date & Time

Wind Direction	Wind Speed
Coordinates	Temperature
Waves	Sky
Forecast	Motoring
Fuel	Water
Captain	Engine Hours

Sea Strength: Calm ● | 1 | 2 | 3 | 4 | 5 | ● Rough

Crew

Notes

Logged By: _____

Date: _____

Departure Location	Departure Time
Stopover	Time
Arrival Location	Date & Time

Wind Direction	Wind Speed
Coordinates	Temperature
Waves	Sky
Forecast	Motoring
Fuel	Water
Captain	Engine Hours

Sea Strength: Calm ● — 1 — 2 — 3 — 4 — 5 — ● Rough

Crew

Notes

Logged By: _____

Date: _____

Departure Location	Departure Time
Stopover	Time
Arrival Location	Date & Time

Wind Direction	Wind Speed
Coordinates	Temperature
Waves	Sky
Forecast	Motoring
Fuel	Water
Captain	Engine Hours

Sea Strength: Calm ●——(1 | 2 | 3 | 4 | 5)——● Rough

Crew

Notes

Logged By: _____

Date:

Departure Location	Departure Time
Stopover	Time
Arrival Location	Date & Time

Wind Direction	Wind Speed
Coordinates	Temperature
Waves	Sky
Forecast	Motoring
Fuel	Water
Captain	Engine Hours

Sea Strength: Calm — 1 2 3 4 5 — Rough

Crew

Notes

Logged By:

Date: _____

Departure Location	Departure Time
Stopover	Time
Arrival Location	Date & Time

Wind Direction	Wind Speed
Coordinates	Temperature
Waves	Sky
Forecast	Motoring
Fuel	Water
Captain	Engine Hours

Sea Strength: Calm ●— 1 | 2 | 3 | 4 | 5 —● Rough

Crew

Notes

Logged By: _____

Date:

Departure Location	Departure Time
Stopover	Time
Arrival Location	Date & Time

Wind Direction	Wind Speed
Coordinates	Temperature
Waves	Sky
Forecast	Motoring
Fuel	Water
Captain	Engine Hours

Sea Strength: Calm ●—○ 1 | 2 | 3 | 4 | 5 —● Rough

Crew

Notes

Logged By:

Date: _____

Departure Location	Departure Time
Stopover	Time
Arrival Location	Date & Time

Wind Direction	Wind Speed
Coordinates	Temperature
Waves	Sky
Forecast	Motoring
Fuel	Water
Captain	Engine Hours

Sea Strength: Calm ●— 1 | 2 | 3 | 4 | 5 —● Rough

Crew

Notes

Logged By: _____

Date: _____

Departure Location	Departure Time
Stopover	Time
Arrival Location	Date & Time

Wind Direction	Wind Speed
Coordinates	Temperature
Waves	Sky
Forecast	Motoring
Fuel	Water
Captain	Engine Hours

Sea Strength: Calm ●━ | 1 | 2 | 3 | 4 | 5 | ━● Rough

Crew

Notes

Logged By: _____

Date: _____

Departure Location	Departure Time
Stopover	Time
Arrival Location	Date & Time

Wind Direction	Wind Speed
Coordinates	Temperature
Waves	Sky
Forecast	Motoring
Fuel	Water
Captain	Engine Hours

Sea Strength: Calm ●—(1 | 2 | 3 | 4 | 5)—● Rough

Crew

Notes

Logged By: _____

Date:

Departure Location	Departure Time
Stopover	Time
Arrival Location	Date & Time

Wind Direction	Wind Speed
Coordinates	Temperature
Waves	Sky
Forecast	Motoring
Fuel	Water
Captain	Engine Hours

Sea Strength: Calm — 1 2 3 4 5 — Rough

Crew

Notes

Logged By:

Date:

Departure Location	Departure Time
Stopover	Time
Arrival Location	Date & Time

Wind Direction	Wind Speed
Coordinates	Temperature
Waves	Sky
Forecast	Motoring
Fuel	Water
Captain	Engine Hours

Sea Strength: Calm ● — 1 2 3 4 5 — ● Rough

Crew

Notes

Logged By:

Date:

Departure Location	Departure Time
Stopover	Time
Arrival Location	Date & Time

Wind Direction	Wind Speed
Coordinates	Temperature
Waves	Sky
Forecast	Motoring
Fuel	Water
Captain	Engine Hours

Sea Strength: Calm — 1 2 3 4 5 — Rough

Crew

Notes

Logged By:

Date: _____

Departure Location	Departure Time
Stopover	Time
Arrival Location	Date & Time

Wind Direction	Wind Speed
Coordinates	Temperature
Waves	Sky
Forecast	Motoring
Fuel	Water
Captain	Engine Hours

Sea Strength: Calm ● ─ | 1 | 2 | 3 | 4 | 5 | ─ ● Rough

Crew

Notes

Logged By: _____

Date:

Departure Location	Departure Time
Stopover	Time
Arrival Location	Date & Time

Wind Direction	Wind Speed
Coordinates	Temperature
Waves	Sky
Forecast	Motoring
Fuel	Water
Captain	Engine Hours

Sea Strength: Calm ●─(1 | 2 | 3 | 4 | 5)─● Rough

Crew

Notes

Logged By:

Date: _____

Departure Location	Departure Time
Stopover	Time
Arrival Location	Date & Time

Wind Direction	Wind Speed
Coordinates	Temperature
Waves	Sky
Forecast	Motoring
Fuel	Water
Captain	Engine Hours

Sea Strength: Calm ●—[1 | 2 | 3 | 4 | 5]—● Rough

Crew

Notes

Logged By: _____

Date: _____

Departure Location	Departure Time
Stopover	Time
Arrival Location	Date & Time

Wind Direction	Wind Speed
Coordinates	Temperature
Waves	Sky
Forecast	Motoring
Fuel	Water
Captain	Engine Hours

Sea Strength: Calm ● — 1 | 2 | 3 | 4 | 5 — ● Rough

Crew

Notes

Logged By: _____

Date: _____

Departure Location	Departure Time
Stopover	Time
Arrival Location	Date & Time

Wind Direction	Wind Speed
Coordinates	Temperature
Waves	Sky
Forecast	Motoring
Fuel	Water
Captain	Engine Hours

Sea Strength: Calm ● 1 2 3 4 5 ● Rough

Crew

Notes

Logged By: _____

Date:

Departure Location	Departure Time
Stopover	Time
Arrival Location	Date & Time

Wind Direction	Wind Speed
Coordinates	Temperature
Waves	Sky
Forecast	Motoring
Fuel	Water
Captain	Engine Hours

Sea Strength: Calm ●———— 1 | 2 | 3 | 4 | 5 ————● Rough

Crew

Notes

Logged By:

Date: _____

Departure Location	Departure Time
Stopover	Time
Arrival Location	Date & Time

Wind Direction	Wind Speed
Coordinates	Temperature
Waves	Sky
Forecast	Motoring
Fuel	Water
Captain	Engine Hours

Sea Strength: Calm •— 1 | 2 | 3 | 4 | 5 —• Rough

Crew

Notes

Logged By: _____

Date: _____

Departure Location	Departure Time
Stopover	Time
Arrival Location	Date & Time

Wind Direction	Wind Speed
Coordinates	Temperature
Waves	Sky
Forecast	Motoring
Fuel	Water
Captain	Engine Hours

Sea Strength: Calm — 1 2 3 4 5 — Rough

Crew

Notes

Logged By: _____

Date: _____

Departure Location	Departure Time
Stopover	Time
Arrival Location	Date & Time

Wind Direction	Wind Speed
Coordinates	Temperature
Waves	Sky
Forecast	Motoring
Fuel	Water
Captain	Engine Hours

Sea Strength: Calm —◯— 1 | 2 | 3 | 4 | 5 —◯ Rough

Crew

Notes

Logged By: _____

Date:

Departure Location	Departure Time
Stopover	Time
Arrival Location	Date & Time

Wind Direction	Wind Speed
Coordinates	Temperature
Waves	Sky
Forecast	Motoring
Fuel	Water
Captain	Engine Hours

Sea Strength: Calm — 1 | 2 | 3 | 4 | 5 — Rough

Crew

Notes

Logged By:

Date: _____

Departure Location	Departure Time
Stopover	Time
Arrival Location	Date & Time

Wind Direction	Wind Speed
Coordinates	Temperature
Waves	Sky
Forecast	Motoring
Fuel	Water
Captain	Engine Hours

Sea Strength: Calm —○— | 1 | 2 | 3 | 4 | 5 | —●— Rough

Crew

Notes

Logged By: _____

Date: _____

Departure Location	Departure Time
Stopover	Time
Arrival Location	Date & Time

Wind Direction	Wind Speed
Coordinates	Temperature
Waves	Sky
Forecast	Motoring
Fuel	Water
Captain	Engine Hours

Sea Strength: Calm — 1 2 3 4 5 — Rough

Crew

Notes

Logged By: _____

Date: _____

Departure Location	Departure Time
Stopover	Time
Arrival Location	Date & Time

Wind Direction	Wind Speed
Coordinates	Temperature
Waves	Sky
Forecast	Motoring
Fuel	Water
Captain	Engine Hours

Sea Strength: Calm ● — 1 — 2 — 3 — 4 — 5 — ● Rough

Crew

Notes

Logged By: _____

Date:

Departure Location	Departure Time
Stopover	Time
Arrival Location	Date & Time

Wind Direction	Wind Speed
Coordinates	Temperature
Waves	Sky
Forecast	Motoring
Fuel	Water
Captain	Engine Hours

Sea Strength: Calm ● 1 2 3 4 5 ● Rough

Crew

Notes

Logged By:

Date: _____

Departure Location	Departure Time
Stopover	Time
Arrival Location	Date & Time

Wind Direction	Wind Speed
Coordinates	Temperature
Waves	Sky
Forecast	Motoring
Fuel	Water
Captain	Engine Hours

Sea Strength: Calm ●— 1 2 3 4 5 —● Rough

Crew

Notes

Logged By: _____

Date: _____

Departure Location	Departure Time
Stopover	Time
Arrival Location	Date & Time

Wind Direction	Wind Speed
Coordinates	Temperature
Waves	Sky
Forecast	Motoring
Fuel	Water
Captain	Engine Hours

Sea Strength: Calm ●——[| 1 | 2 | 3 | 4 | 5]——● Rough

Crew

Notes

Logged By: _____

Date: _____

Departure Location	Departure Time
Stopover	Time
Arrival Location	Date & Time

Wind Direction	Wind Speed
Coordinates	Temperature
Waves	Sky
Forecast	Motoring
Fuel	Water
Captain	Engine Hours

Sea Strength: Calm — 1 — 2 — 3 — 4 — 5 — Rough

Crew

Notes

Logged By: _____

Date:

Departure Location	Departure Time
Stopover	Time
Arrival Location	Date & Time

Wind Direction	Wind Speed
Coordinates	Temperature
Waves	Sky
Forecast	Motoring
Fuel	Water
Captain	Engine Hours

Sea Strength: Calm ● 1 2 3 4 5 ● Rough

Crew

Notes

Logged By:

Date: _____

Departure Location		Departure Time	
Stopover		Time	
Arrival Location		Date & Time	

Wind Direction	Wind Speed
Coordinates	Temperature
Waves	Sky
Forecast	Motoring
Fuel	Water
Captain	Engine Hours

Sea Strength: Calm ●———— 1 | 2 | 3 | 4 | 5 ————● Rough

Crew

Notes

Logged By: _____

Date:

Departure Location	Departure Time
Stopover	Time
Arrival Location	Date & Time

Wind Direction	Wind Speed
Coordinates	Temperature
Waves	Sky
Forecast	Motoring
Fuel	Water
Captain	Engine Hours

Sea Strength: Calm — 1 2 3 4 5 — Rough

Crew

Notes

Logged By:

Date:

Departure Location	Departure Time
Stopover	Time
Arrival Location	Date & Time

Wind Direction	Wind Speed
Coordinates	Temperature
Waves	Sky
Forecast	Motoring
Fuel	Water
Captain	Engine Hours

Sea Strength: Calm — 1 2 3 4 5 — Rough

Crew

Notes

Logged By:

Date:

Departure Location	Departure Time
Stopover	Time
Arrival Location	Date & Time

Wind Direction	Wind Speed
Coordinates	Temperature
Waves	Sky
Forecast	Motoring
Fuel	Water
Captain	Engine Hours

Sea Strength: Calm — 1 2 3 4 5 — Rough

Crew

Notes

Logged By:

Date: _____

Departure Location	Departure Time
Stopover	Time
Arrival Location	Date & Time

Wind Direction	Wind Speed
Coordinates	Temperature
Waves	Sky
Forecast	Motoring
Fuel	Water
Captain	Engine Hours

Sea Strength: Calm ● — 1 | 2 | 3 | 4 | 5 — ● Rough

Crew

Notes

Logged By: _____

Date: _____

Departure Location		Departure Time
Stopover		Time
Arrival Location		Date & Time

Wind Direction	Wind Speed
Coordinates	Temperature
Waves	Sky
Forecast	Motoring
Fuel	Water
Captain	Engine Hours

Sea Strength: Calm ●— | 1 | 2 | 3 | 4 | 5 | —● Rough

Crew

Notes

Logged By: _____

Date: _____

Departure Location	Departure Time
Stopover	Time
Arrival Location	Date & Time

Wind Direction	Wind Speed
Coordinates	Temperature
Waves	Sky
Forecast	Motoring
Fuel	Water
Captain	Engine Hours

Sea Strength: Calm ●———— 1 | 2 | 3 | 4 | 5 ————● Rough

Crew

Notes

Logged By: _____

Date: _____

Departure Location	Departure Time
Stopover	Time
Arrival Location	Date & Time

Wind Direction	Wind Speed
Coordinates	Temperature
Waves	Sky
Forecast	Motoring
Fuel	Water
Captain	Engine Hours

Sea Strength: Calm ●———[1 | 2 | 3 | 4 | 5]———● Rough

Crew

Notes

Logged By: _____

Date:

Departure Location	Departure Time
Stopover	Time
Arrival Location	Date & Time

Wind Direction	Wind Speed
Coordinates	Temperature
Waves	Sky
Forecast	Motoring
Fuel	Water
Captain	Engine Hours

Sea Strength: Calm — | 1 | 2 | 3 | 4 | 5 | — Rough

Crew

Notes

Logged By:

Date: _____

Departure Location		Departure Time
Stopover		Time
Arrival Location		Date & Time

Wind Direction	Wind Speed
Coordinates	Temperature
Waves	Sky
Forecast	Motoring
Fuel	Water
Captain	Engine Hours

Sea Strength: Calm● 1 2 3 4 5 ●Rough

Crew

Notes

Logged By: _____

Date: _____

Departure Location	Departure Time
Stopover	Time
Arrival Location	Date & Time

Wind Direction	Wind Speed
Coordinates	Temperature
Waves	Sky
Forecast	Motoring
Fuel	Water
Captain	Engine Hours

Sea Strength: Calm —○— 1 | 2 | 3 | 4 | 5 —● Rough

Crew

Notes

Logged By: _____

Date:

Departure Location	Departure Time
Stopover	Time
Arrival Location	Date & Time

Wind Direction	Wind Speed
Coordinates	Temperature
Waves	Sky
Forecast	Motoring
Fuel	Water
Captain	Engine Hours

Sea Strength: Calm ● — 1 | 2 | 3 | 4 | 5 — ● Rough

Crew

Notes

Logged By:

Date:

Departure Location	Departure Time
Stopover	Time
Arrival Location	Date & Time

Wind Direction	Wind Speed
Coordinates	Temperature
Waves	Sky
Forecast	Motoring
Fuel	Water
Captain	Engine Hours

Sea Strength: Calm —— 1 2 3 4 5 —— Rough

Crew

Notes

Logged By:

Date:

Departure Location	Departure Time
Stopover	Time
Arrival Location	Date & Time

Wind Direction	Wind Speed
Coordinates	Temperature
Waves	Sky
Forecast	Motoring
Fuel	Water
Captain	Engine Hours

Sea Strength: Calm — 1 2 3 4 5 — Rough

Crew

Notes

Logged By:

Date: _____

Departure Location	Departure Time
Stopover	Time
Arrival Location	Date & Time

Wind Direction	Wind Speed
Coordinates	Temperature
Waves	Sky
Forecast	Motoring
Fuel	Water
Captain	Engine Hours

Sea Strength: Calm ● — 1 | 2 | 3 | 4 | 5 — ● Rough

Crew

Notes

Logged By: _____

Date:

Departure Location	Departure Time
Stopover	Time
Arrival Location	Date & Time

Wind Direction	Wind Speed
Coordinates	Temperature
Waves	Sky
Forecast	Motoring
Fuel	Water
Captain	Engine Hours

Sea Strength: Calm ●— 1 2 3 4 5 —● Rough

Crew

Notes

Logged By:

Date: _____

Departure Location	Departure Time
Stopover	Time
Arrival Location	Date & Time

Wind Direction	Wind Speed
Coordinates	Temperature
Waves	Sky
Forecast	Motoring
Fuel	Water
Captain	Engine Hours

Sea Strength: Calm ●—◯ 1 | 2 | 3 | 4 | 5 —● Rough

Crew

Notes

Logged By: _____

Date:

Departure Location	Departure Time
Stopover	Time
Arrival Location	Date & Time

Wind Direction	Wind Speed
Coordinates	Temperature
Waves	Sky
Forecast	Motoring
Fuel	Water
Captain	Engine Hours

Sea Strength: Calm ● — 1 2 3 4 5 — ● Rough

Crew

Notes

Logged By:

Date:

Departure Location	Departure Time
Stopover	Time
Arrival Location	Date & Time

Wind Direction	Wind Speed
Coordinates	Temperature
Waves	Sky
Forecast	Motoring
Fuel	Water
Captain	Engine Hours

Sea Strength: Calm ● 1 2 3 4 5 ● Rough

Crew

Notes

Logged By:

Date:

Departure Location	Departure Time
Stopover	Time
Arrival Location	Date & Time

Wind Direction	Wind Speed
Coordinates	Temperature
Waves	Sky
Forecast	Motoring
Fuel	Water
Captain	Engine Hours

Sea Strength: Calm — 1 2 3 4 5 — Rough

Crew

Notes

Logged By:

Date: _____

Departure Location	Departure Time
Stopover	Time
Arrival Location	Date & Time

Wind Direction	Wind Speed
Coordinates	Temperature
Waves	Sky
Forecast	Motoring
Fuel	Water
Captain	Engine Hours

Sea Strength: Calm ●————— 1 | 2 | 3 | 4 | 5 —————● Rough

Crew

Notes

Logged By: _____

Date: _____

Departure Location		Departure Time
Stopover		Time
Arrival Location		Date & Time

Wind Direction	Wind Speed
Coordinates	Temperature
Waves	Sky
Forecast	Motoring
Fuel	Water
Captain	Engine Hours

Sea Strength: Calm ●━━ | 1 | 2 | 3 | 4 | 5 | ━● Rough

Crew

Notes

Logged By: _____

Date: _____

Departure Location	Departure Time
Stopover	Time
Arrival Location	Date & Time

Wind Direction	Wind Speed
Coordinates	Temperature
Waves	Sky
Forecast	Motoring
Fuel	Water
Captain	Engine Hours

Sea Strength: Calm — 1 2 3 4 5 — Rough

Crew

Notes

Logged By: _____

Date:

Departure Location	Departure Time
Stopover	Time
Arrival Location	Date & Time

Wind Direction	Wind Speed
Coordinates	Temperature
Waves	Sky
Forecast	Motoring
Fuel	Water
Captain	Engine Hours

Sea Strength: Calm — 1 2 3 4 5 — Rough

Crew

Notes

Logged By:

Date: _____

Departure Location	Departure Time
Stopover	Time
Arrival Location	Date & Time

Wind Direction	Wind Speed
Coordinates	Temperature
Waves	Sky
Forecast	Motoring
Fuel	Water
Captain	Engine Hours

Sea Strength: Calm — | 1 | 2 | 3 | 4 | 5 | — Rough

Crew

Notes

Logged By: _____

Date: _____

Departure Location	Departure Time
Stopover	Time
Arrival Location	Date & Time

Wind Direction	Wind Speed
Coordinates	Temperature
Waves	Sky
Forecast	Motoring
Fuel	Water
Captain	Engine Hours

Sea Strength: Calm ●———[1 | 2 | 3 | 4 | 5]———● Rough

Crew

Notes

Logged By: _____

Date:

Departure Location	Departure Time
Stopover	Time
Arrival Location	Date & Time

Wind Direction	Wind Speed
Coordinates	Temperature
Waves	Sky
Forecast	Motoring
Fuel	Water
Captain	Engine Hours

Sea Strength: Calm   1   2   3   4   5   Rough

Crew

Notes

Logged By:

Date:

Departure Location	Departure Time
Stopover	Time
Arrival Location	Date & Time

Wind Direction	Wind Speed
Coordinates	Temperature
Waves	Sky
Forecast	Motoring
Fuel	Water
Captain	Engine Hours

Sea Strength: Calm ● — 1 | 2 | 3 | 4 | 5 — ● Rough

Crew

Notes

Logged By:

Date: _____

Departure Location	Departure Time
Stopover	Time
Arrival Location	Date & Time

Wind Direction	Wind Speed
Coordinates	Temperature
Waves	Sky
Forecast	Motoring
Fuel	Water
Captain	Engine Hours

Sea Strength: Calm ● — | 1 | 2 | 3 | 4 | 5 | — ● Rough

Crew

Notes

Logged By: _____

Date: _____

Departure Location	Departure Time
Stopover	Time
Arrival Location	Date & Time

Wind Direction	Wind Speed
Coordinates	Temperature
Waves	Sky
Forecast	Motoring
Fuel	Water
Captain	Engine Hours

Sea Strength: Calm —◯— 1 | 2 | 3 | 4 | 5 —● Rough

Crew

Notes

Logged By: _____

Date:

Departure Location	Departure Time
Stopover	Time
Arrival Location	Date & Time

Wind Direction	Wind Speed
Coordinates	Temperature
Waves	Sky
Forecast	Motoring
Fuel	Water
Captain	Engine Hours

Sea Strength: Calm — 1 2 3 4 5 — Rough

Crew

Notes

Logged By:

Date:

Departure Location	Departure Time
Stopover	Time
Arrival Location	Date & Time

Wind Direction	Wind Speed
Coordinates	Temperature
Waves	Sky
Forecast	Motoring
Fuel	Water
Captain	Engine Hours

Sea Strength: Calm — 1 2 3 4 5 — Rough

Crew

Notes

Logged By:

Date: _____

Departure Location	Departure Time
Stopover	Time
Arrival Location	Date & Time

Wind Direction	Wind Speed
Coordinates	Temperature
Waves	Sky
Forecast	Motoring
Fuel	Water
Captain	Engine Hours

Sea Strength: Calm ●— | 1 | 2 | 3 | 4 | 5 | —● Rough

Crew

Notes

Logged By: _____

Date:

Departure Location	Departure Time
Stopover	Time
Arrival Location	Date & Time

Wind Direction	Wind Speed
Coordinates	Temperature
Waves	Sky
Forecast	Motoring
Fuel	Water
Captain	Engine Hours

Sea Strength: Calm ● —[1 | 2 | 3 | 4 | 5]— ● Rough

Crew

Notes

Logged By:

Date: _____

Departure Location	Departure Time
Stopover	Time
Arrival Location	Date & Time

Wind Direction	Wind Speed
Coordinates	Temperature
Waves	Sky
Forecast	Motoring
Fuel	Water
Captain	Engine Hours

Sea Strength: Calm—[1 | 2 | 3 | 4 | 5]—Rough

Crew

Notes

Logged By: _____

Date:

Departure Location	Departure Time
Stopover	Time
Arrival Location	Date & Time

Wind Direction	Wind Speed
Coordinates	Temperature
Waves	Sky
Forecast	Motoring
Fuel	Water
Captain	Engine Hours

Sea Strength: Calm — 1 2 3 4 5 — Rough

Crew

Notes

Logged By:

Date: _____

Departure Location	Departure Time
Stopover	Time
Arrival Location	Date & Time

Wind Direction	Wind Speed
Coordinates	Temperature
Waves	Sky
Forecast	Motoring
Fuel	Water
Captain	Engine Hours

Sea Strength: Calm ●——| 1 | 2 | 3 | 4 | 5 |——● Rough

Crew

Notes

Logged By: _____

Date: _____

Departure Location	Departure Time
Stopover	Time
Arrival Location	Date & Time

Wind Direction	Wind Speed
Coordinates	Temperature
Waves	Sky
Forecast	Motoring
Fuel	Water
Captain	Engine Hours

Sea Strength: Calm — 1 2 3 4 5 — Rough

Crew

Notes

Logged By: _____

Date:

Departure Location	Departure Time
Stopover	Time
Arrival Location	Date & Time

Wind Direction	Wind Speed
Coordinates	Temperature
Waves	Sky
Forecast	Motoring
Fuel	Water
Captain	Engine Hours

Sea Strength: Calm — 1 2 3 4 5 — Rough

Crew

Notes

Logged By:

Date:

Departure Location	Departure Time
Stopover	Time
Arrival Location	Date & Time

Wind Direction	Wind Speed
Coordinates	Temperature
Waves	Sky
Forecast	Motoring
Fuel	Water
Captain	Engine Hours

Sea Strength: Calm ●—| 1 | 2 | 3 | 4 | 5 |—● Rough

Crew

Notes

Logged By:

Date: _____

Departure Location	Departure Time
Stopover	Time
Arrival Location	Date & Time

Wind Direction	Wind Speed
Coordinates	Temperature
Waves	Sky
Forecast	Motoring
Fuel	Water
Captain	Engine Hours

Sea Strength: Calm — 1 | 2 | 3 | 4 | 5 — Rough

Crew

Notes

Logged By: _____

Date: _____

Departure Location		Departure Time
Stopover		Time
Arrival Location		Date & Time

Wind Direction	Wind Speed
Coordinates	Temperature
Waves	Sky
Forecast	Motoring
Fuel	Water
Captain	Engine Hours

Sea Strength: Calm ●— 1   2   3   4   5 —● Rough

Crew

Notes

Logged By: _____

Date:

Departure Location	Departure Time
Stopover	Time
Arrival Location	Date & Time

Wind Direction	Wind Speed
Coordinates	Temperature
Waves	Sky
Forecast	Motoring
Fuel	Water
Captain	Engine Hours

Sea Strength: Calm — 1 2 3 4 5 — Rough

Crew

Notes

Logged By:

Date:

Departure Location	Departure Time
Stopover	Time
Arrival Location	Date & Time

Wind Direction	Wind Speed
Coordinates	Temperature
Waves	Sky
Forecast	Motoring
Fuel	Water
Captain	Engine Hours

Sea Strength: Calm ● 1 2 3 4 5 ● Rough

Crew

Notes

Logged By:

Date:

Departure Location	Departure Time
Stopover	Time
Arrival Location	Date & Time

Wind Direction	Wind Speed
Coordinates	Temperature
Waves	Sky
Forecast	Motoring
Fuel	Water
Captain	Engine Hours

Sea Strength: Calm — 1 2 3 4 5 — Rough

Crew

Notes

Logged By:

Made in the USA
Thornton, CO
08/20/24 09:26:49

833ce8bc-b693-4ebc-bce5-1622a09d82bfR01